Introducing
SCOTLAND
a pictorial journey

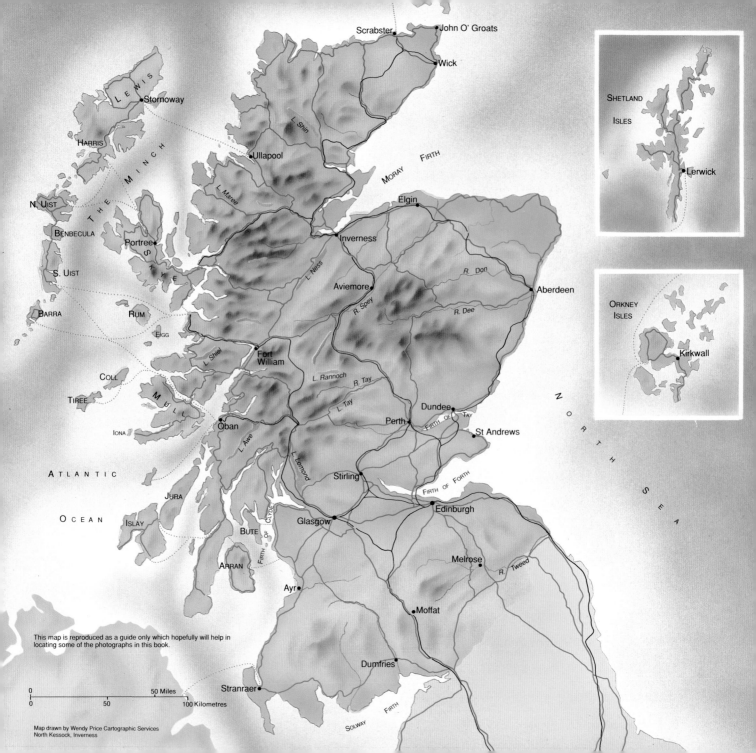

John O' Groats

Scrabster

Wick

SHETLAND
ISLES

Lerwick

L E W I S

Stornoway

HARRIS

T H E   M I N C H

MORAY   FIRTH

Elgin

ORKNEY
ISLES

Kirkwall

Ullapool

L. Shin

N. UIST

BENBECULA

L. Maree

Inverness

R. Don

Aberdeen

Portree

S K Y E

L. Ness

Aviemore

R. Dee

S. UIST

R. Spey

BARRA

RUM

EIGG

N
O
R
T
H

S
E
A

COLL

L. Shiel

Fort
William

L. Rannoch

R. Tay

TIREE

M U L L

L. Tay

Dundee

FIRTH OF TAY

IONA

Oban

L. Awe

Perth

St Andrews

A T L A N T I C

JURA

L. Lomond

Stirling

O C E A N

ISLAY

BUTE

FIRTH OF CLYDE

Glasgow

FIRTH OF FORTH

Edinburgh

ARRAN

Ayr

Melrose

R. Tweed

Moffat

This map is reproduced as a guide only which hopefully will help in
locating some of the photographs in this book.

Dumfries

0   50 Miles

0   50   100 Kilometres

Stranraer

SOLWAY   FIRTH

Map drawn by Wendy Price Cartographic Services
North Kessock, Inverness

INTRODUCING SCOTLAND

a pictorial journey

Scotland is a country of marvellous contrasts and a wide diversity of scenery. From the rolling Borders to the rugged Highlands, and from the Western Isles to the deep east coast firths, it encompasses a stunning variety of scenery and heritage. Long craggy coastlines, rich pastoral landscapes, austere castles, towering mountains and racing rivers all combine to form one of the world's best loved countries for travel.

Scotland covers almost 30,500 square miles, more than 90% of which is classified as countryside. Her population of just over five million resides mainly in the central belt area of Edinburgh and Glasgow, and in the east coast cities of Dundee, Aberdeen and Inverness.

There are no less than 787 islands within Scotland's borders, only a quarter of which are inhabited. These islands include the haunting inner and outer Hebrides where the Atlantic Ocean reaches the sandy, western shores resulting in beautiful azure seas, and the island groups of Orkney and Shetland. These northerly islands are bounded on their eastern shores by the relatively shallow North Sea, where even moderate winds can bring about turbulent seas. In these climes, and indeed along the remainder of Scotland's east coast, great towering cliffs and arches contrast with stretches of dune-backed sandy beaches.

Scotland is a high country. In the Border region, the Southern Upland hills are undulating with rich, arable land in their valleys. Both the rivers Clyde and Tweed have their sources in the Borders. Further north the mountains are more rugged, rising to spectacular peaks, most of which are prefixed with "Ben", the Gaelic for mountain. Britain's highest mountain, Ben Nevis towers above the town of Fort William, and names such as Ben Lomond, Ben MacDui and Ben More are very familiar in the Highlands.

In this pictorial guide, we welcome you to Scotland's scenery and heritage. The beauty of the country is caught through the camera lens as the seasons and landscape change, and we will perhaps give you an indication of Scotland as she presents herself in a season other than the one in which you presently find yourself. We hope you will enjoy your journey through the scenery, and be encouraged to return again to your favourite corners of this beautiful country.

Our journey into Scotland begins in the south-east where the fertile lands of the Borders region welcome the traveller with magnificent views over the Cheviot, Moorfoot and Lammermuir hills to the plain of the central belt. Here, a variety of roads, major and minor, will take you through border towns such as Jedburgh, Melrose, Hawick and Abbotsford. The towns and villages here have witnessed much in the way of strife over the centuries as the borderers fought to repel attackers intent on heading north.

Now the quiet market towns stand proud to welcome visitors among their historic buildings and artifacts. You will find fine examples of Gothic culture in the ruins of Dryburgh and Jedburgh, and Melrose Abbey, rebuilt in the 14th century, is perhaps one of the finest examples of pure Gothic tradition.

On the east coast of the borders you will find the busy fishing ports of Eyemouth and St Abb's. Fishing has been of

Opposite
The Border town of Melrose, set amongst the Eildon hills.

Dramatic lighting across the River Tweed at Peebles.

Jedburgh Abbey ruins, founded by King David I in 1138, the abbey was a place of Augustinian worship for four centuries.

major importance here since the 12th century, and while necessary upgrading has taken place, the towns have maintained their original, attractive characteristics and the coastline presents a mixture of long, dune-covered beaches and high craggy cliffs.

This blend of dramatic coastline and rich countryside continues as the Borders Region ends and you enter the realms of the Lothians. While the landscape flattens as you approach the plain of the Central belt, the Pentland hills and the unmistakable outline of

Edinburgh city viewed from the Queen's Park and Salisbury Crags.

Arthur's Seat in Edinburgh dominate the skyline.

Edinburgh, Scotland's capital city, is beautiful, open and green. It is a city steeped in history, contains a wealth of tourist attractions and hosts one of the world's famous (annual) Arts Festivals. Dominating the city, and impressive from any angle, is the castle. Home to Royalty since the 11th century, the castle is strategically sited on a volcanic rock high above what was then the "old town" of Edinburgh.

The architecture of Edinburgh is rich indeed, and within the centre of the city there are many fascinating and spectacular vistas forever opening up to delight the visitor. Prominent landmarks such as the Scott Monument,

Opposite
The East Lothian seaside resort of North Berwick on the Firth of Forth.

Looking along Edinburgh's Princes Street from Calton Hill.

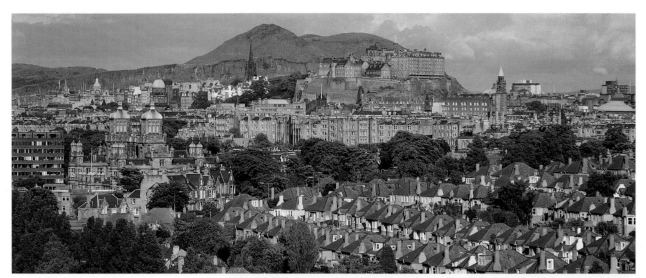

Calton Hill and Nelson's Monument sit amidst beautiful garden greenery, and Princes Street gardens themselves are a magnificent feature within the city.

Edinburgh is split into two - the Old and New Towns. The Old Town stretches from the castle to Holyrood Palace down what is known as the Royal Mile, which

Above
The city of Edinburgh from the west including Arthur's Seat.

Right
Ramsay Gardens at the top of The Mound, viewed from Princes Street.

Opposite
Edinburgh Castle and St. Cuthbert's Church at dusk.

The world famous Forth Rail Bridge carries trains across the Firth of Forth connecting the Lothians with Fife.

encompasses an alluring maze of courtyards and closes each with its own story (and occasionally a ghost). The Georgian New Town stretches across the North Bridge and was planned as a succession of elegant streets and splendid squares, the most notable of which, Charlotte Square, was designed by the architect Robert Adam.

Edinburgh bustles with visitors all year round, and there are many ways to enjoy the myriad of attractions and visitor centres in and around the city.

Crossing the Firth of Forth into Fife takes the traveller into the Central Lowlands of Scotland. The northern coastline of the Forth, the East Neuk, is dotted with a delightful series of fishing villages, each clustered round its own harbour. The villages; Crail, Anstruther, Pittenweem and St Monace are a joy to discover. Their history also dates back to the 10th/11th centuries when Fife was at the hub of the nation, with Dunfermline as the political centre of Scotland and St Andrews as the Ecclesiastical. In the heroic days of the great sailing clippers, when every day

Above
The Fife village of Pittenweem and the typical rocky coastline.

Below
The University town of St. Andrews, home of golf and learning since the 15th century.

Below
16-17th century houses at Culross, a former Royal Burgh in the Kingdom of Fife.

counted, an East Neuk skipper held the all time record of 83 days to sail a ship from Gravesend to Hong Kong.

The town of Dunfermline with its great Abbey, where Kings of Scotland were crowned, and its Royal residential Palace figures largely in Scottish history . One of Dunfermline's famous boys was the steel baron and multi millionaire, Andrew Carnegie

Left
Looking over the city of Dundee towards Fife with the Tay Road Bridge spanning the river.

Below
Looking back across the Tay estuary towards Dundee and Angus.

who spent much of his fortune on public benefactions.

At the head of the Forth is the town of Stirling, where again a castle dominates the visitor's approach to the town. Stirling was an important Scottish stronghold, and proof of this is the numerous battles fought in its vicinity; Stirling Bridge 1297, Falkirk 1298 and 1766, Bannockburn 1314, Sauchieburn 1488, Kilsyth 1645 and Sherrifmuir in 1715.

Much of the interior of Fife contains further villages of historic importance, and associations with the trades which grew up in the area. The beautiful burgh of Culross (pronounced Koo-ross) has undergone a programme of restoration to ensure the preservation of its typically Scottish architectural charm, where pedimented dormer windows and door trims, gable ends and crow stepping blend with decorative finials and inscribed lintels and forestairs.

Glamis Castle, the childhood home of Her Majesty Queen Elizabeth, The Queen Mother.

A colourful evening view of Arbroath harbour, home of the famous Smokie, a smoked haddock.

In Fife you will find the world famous Royal and Ancient golf club at St Andrews. Set on the spectacular North Sea coast, this busy tourist town is also a great seat of learning with its 15th century university.

The north coast of Fife marks the end of the Central Lowlands and brings the traveller to the Firth of Tay and the start of the Highlands. Perth, the "fair city" on the Tay has succeeded in retaining the atmosphere of a county town.

Situated at the head of the Firth and at the mouth of the river Tay, Perth remains important as a communications centre of bus, road and rail transport. Roman camps were situated in and around Perth, but the first community grew up around the inland port at the head of the river. Perth is also a centre of agricultural shows and in particular has links with Aberdeen Angus and Highland Cattle Associations.

In Perthshire the visitor encounters a splendid array of scenery encompassing fertile hills littered with a wonderful array of lochs and castles. Towns and villages such as Aberfeldy and Crieff with its links

as a Victorian spa town are well worth exploring.

Quiet roads will take the visitor through lush glens to the shores of Loch Tay where Ben Lawyers rises to majestic

Opposite *The city of Perth on the banks of the R. Tay and Drummond Castle gardens near Crieff.*

Above *The Falls of Dochart at Killin and the picturesque Strathfillan in winter.*

heights on the north shore. Throughout its fourteen miles, the loch never extends to more than one mile in width. At the head of Loch Tay is the scenic village of Killin, where the river Dochart tumbles as rapids into the Falls of Dochart, before feeding into the loch itself.

The area southeast of Perthshire, known as the Trossachs, conjures up an idyllic

landscape of great scenic beauty. Rugged, but not so lofty, mountains and their wooded slopes lead down to the sparkling waters of Loch Katrine, Loch Achray, Loch Venacher and Loch Lomond. The proximity of the Trossachs to the urban populations of Glasgow and Edinburgh make it a popular place for locals and visitors alike.

Set in the beautiful Tummel

Opposite
The Perthshire village of Fortingall, birthplace of Pontius Pilate and home to the oldest yew tree in Britain.

Above
Beautiful Loch Tummel near Pitlochry was a favourite of Queen Victoria. The peaceful village of Kenmore by Loch Tay.

Valley, the town of Pitlochry makes an ideal touring centre. Pitlochry is set close to Loch Faskally where a large hydro electric dam retains the waters as part of the Tummel Valley scheme. A salmon ladder on the loch allows salmon to move upstream during their spawning season.

The road and railway routes leading to Lochs Tummel and Rannoch run parallel to negotiate the narrow pass of Killiecrankie. The battle of Killiecrankie, fought between the mainly Highland Jacobite army and government troops, was brief and ended in victory for the Jacobites.

From Perthshire our journey moves north over the heights of Drumochter summit. At more than 1,000 ft above sea-level, the landscape is barren but nonetheless impressive. To the west are the huge U-shaped valleys of Rannoch Moor, gouged out as glaciers retreated. This desolate wilderness, which has an average height of 1,000 ft, is centred round the glens of Rannoch, Tummel and Glencoe.

To the east, the Cairngorm mountains present themselves as once again the landscape becomes more fertile and the road reaches down to the highland capital of Inverness.

The coastal route north east from Perth takes the visitor towards Aberdeen and Peterhead. The northern shores of the Firth of Tay are famous for fruit growing, and in the summer months the air is rich

Above
A view towards Pitlochry in Perthshire.

Above right
Autumn comes to the still waters of Loch Achray in the Trossachs.

Right
A summer view of Blair Castle near Blair Atholl, home of The Atholl Highlanders, the only private army in the British Isles.

with sweet-smelling strawberries and the famous tayberries. This shoreline leads to the city of Dundee. With the introduction of the steamship in the 1860s, Dundee, along with Peterhead, took over from Hull in leading Britain's whaling and seal fisheries. The oil found a ready market in the jute mills of Dundee and the whaling industry continued until the onset of the first world war.

Dundee was famous for the three "Js", jute as mentioned above, jam (and marmalade) and journalism. The famous DC Thomson newspaper empire is situated in the city, and characters such as Desperate Dan, Dennis the Menace and Korky the Kat were all born here.

The journey along the coastline continues through towns such as Arbroath and Montrose where agriculture and fishing have blended happily together through the centuries, and where these industries

Top right *The Cairngorm mountains viewed from Rothiemurchus Estate in Speyside.*

Right *Loch Morlich and its sandy beach is a popular watersports centre near Aviemore.*

Ruthven Barracks near Kingussie in the Spey Valley were destroyed by the Jacobites in 1746.

The lovely Victorian buildings of Tormore Distillery near Grantown on Spey.

today still merge comfortably with tourism and history.

Further inland the roads begin to climb over the Grampian Mountains, and into Deeside. The River Dee, rich in salmon, flows from its 4,000 foot source, through the wild Lairig Ghru and due east to the sea at Aberdeen.

Within the hills and glens are many fine castles, not least of those associated with Royalty which have given the area its title "Royal Deeside".

The city of Aberdeen lies between the rivers of Don and Dee. The present city, developed from two separate fishing villages, is backed by a rich, agricultural hinterland and has become the offshore capital of Europe. Much of the city's architecture has involved the use of fully dressed granite,

giving rise to the title, "the granite city." Aberdeen's maritime past includes shipbuilding for whaling and that most graceful of boats the tea-clipper.

The River Spey, whilst having her source far to the west, becomes dominant to the northeast of the Cairngorms, and this is of course the land of whisky. Distilleries, large and small, abound in quiet and unspoilt glens. Names like Glenfiddich, Glenlivet and Tamdhu bring a welcome twitch to the whisky-

The Highland capital of Inverness on the banks of the R Ness. Inverness is situated at the northern end of the Great Glen and the Caledonian Canal.

lover's nostril, and many happy (non-driving) hours should be spent exploring the proliferation of distilleries on offer.

Inverness stands at the north end of the Great Glen, one of the world's best known geological faultlines. At the very hub of the Highlands' communications systems, the town makes an ideal touring centre for much of

town centre.

The Great Glen splits Scotland in two from Inverness in the North to Fort William in the south. This magnificent glen was formed millions of years ago when the northern part of the Caledonian mountains "slid" more than 60 miles to the south. The resultant wide glen with its three freshwater lochs provides a breathtaking panorama throughout its 65 miles. The most famous Loch is of course Loch Ness, whose dark depths house the monster, "Nessie."

the Highlands. The strategic importance of the town has been appreciated from earliest times, and a series of castles preceded the one you will now see standing proudly above the

General Wade's military road passes through the Great Glen over The Old Bridge at Invermoriston which was designed by Thomas Telford.

Boats navigate through the lock gates on the Caledonian Canal at Fort Augustus, the southernmost end of Loch Ness.

Opposite
Urquhart Castle and Loch Ness. The castle was seized by Robert the Bruce in 1307 and much later suffered bombardment during the Jacobite Rebellion.

The Ring of Brodgar on Orkney.

Photo: Charles Tait

The Isle of Jura from Gigha, Argyll

Kerrycroy village, Isle of Bute

Castlebay harbour, Isle of Barra

Photo: Charles Tait

Seilebost beach on Harris, Western Isles

Photo: Charles Tait

Port of Ness, Isle of Lewis

Scalloway on the northern Isle of Shetland

dscapes

Goat Fell (874m) and village of Lamlash, Arran

Traditional thatched croft house, Isle of Tiree

Northton village, South Harris

Port Askaig on the Isle of Islay

Snow capped peaks of the Isle of Rhum

Sheep shearing on South Uist, Hebrides

Photo: Charles Tait

Photo: A McKenna

Photo: Charles Tait

The engineer Thomas Telford used these three lochs as the basis for his design of the Caledonian Canal which, when it was completed in 1822, was the first canal to carry ships from one coast of Britain to the other.

To the north and east of the Great Glen the road follows the coastline round the firths of Moray, Cromarty, Beauly and Dornoch up to the wild, exposed shores of Caithness and Sutherland. Contrary to its name, the Black Isle on the northern shores of the Moray Firth is an area of outstanding fertility and natural rural charm. Further along the coastline you are in the lands of the Sutherlands. Their ancestral home, Dunrobin Castle, stands impressively overlooking the sea.

Fishing continues to be

Scotland's NE coast is dotted with towns and villages. Stonehaven harbour and town lie just south of Aberdeen and the tiny village of Pennan sits snugly at the bottom of cliffs.

important along this imposing coastline and the most northerly shores of the mainland. The town of Wick was one of the first in Britain to develop the herring industry on a large scale,

and Scrabster continues to provide important harbour facilities as well as being the starting point for a trip to the Orkneys.

The very north of Britain's mainland is a land of contrasts. Bleak moorlands lead to miles of breathtaking, dune covered beaches where huge seas pound ashore. There are many viewpoints along this coastline

Balmoral Castle in Deeside has been the summer residence of the Royal Family since the days of Queen Victoria and Prince Albert.

A winter scene on the R Dee from Invercauld Bridge near Braemar.

The city of Aberdeen celebrates the visit of one of the largest surviving sailing ships in the world.

Photo: Charles Tait

where the vista across the sea
to the Orkney Islands compares
favourably with views inland to
the mountains of Ben Hope and
Ben Loyal.

The archipelago of the
Orkneys is made up of 67
islands, fewer than 30 of which
are inhabited. The first settlers
were established on the islands

in the fourth millennium BC and
there is a great wealth of
prehistoric remains to be
discovered at Skara Brae, Maes
Howe, the standing stones at
Brodgar and many iron age
brochs. These islands being low
lying and fertile mean that
agriculture is a principal source
of income with beef cattle and

dairying being the main
activities. Distilling and tourism
also provide much income for
the islanders.

The Orkney Islands have a
wealth of attractions to offer the
unhurried visitor, from the staggering cliffs where great stacks
such as "the Old Man of Hoy"
tower from the sea, to peaceful,

pastoral landscapes filled with wildlife.

The most northerly of Scotlands, 60 miles north of Orkney, are the Shetlands 100 islands of which only 20 are inhabited. In contrast with Orkney, Shetland has few tracts of fertile, flat land and is deeply penetrated by the sea. The main economic activities of crofting and fishing have been added to over the past twenty years by the arrival of the oil industry. Sullom Voe houses Europe's largest oil terminal and now ranks after fishing as the second largest employer in the islands. You will never be far from the sea in Shetland, and the islands retain the attractions of wild beauty, solitude and empty spaces.

Scotland's north west coast is indented with great sea lochs which cut deeply into some of

Castle Sinclair looks out to sea on Noss Head near the northern town of Wick in Caithness.

The last house in mainland Britain at John O Groats.

Opposite
'St Ola' sails past the Old Man of Hoy (137m) on Orkney.

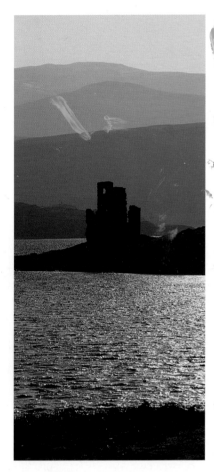

Loch Assynt and Ardvreck Castle with the distant hills of Sutherland.

Evening light over Ben Loyal (764m) seen from across the Kyle of Tongue.

The dominant mountain Stac Polly (613m) Sutherland, in winter.

Opposite
The remote mountainous area of Sutherland with Loch Stack and Ben Arkle (787m).

Europe's wildest and most remote peninsulas. Outstanding, isolated peaks such as Suilven,

Slioch (980m) towers above the beautiful Loch Maree in Wester Ross.

From the summit of Bealach Nam Bo looking down towards Loch Kishorn and the village of Kishorn.

Opposite
The tiny village of Shieldaig by Loch Shieldaig is overshadowed by the impressive Liathach (1054m) in the Torridon area of Wester Ross.

Quinag and Ben Hope dominate the landscape across wide and beautiful plateaux. A journey down the west coast from Britain's most north westerly mainland point, Cape Wrath, will take you through awe-inspiring and rugged scenery. From the fishing villages of Kinlochbervie and Lochinver to Loch Broom where a huge gorge leads to the pic- turesque town of Ullapool.

Here fishing and tourism live happily side by side and large Russian Klondykers ply their trade.

This coast of Scotland benefits from the effects of the Gulf Stream, and the temperate climate allows feats of outstand-ing horticulture not generally expected in such northerly climes. The National Trust have harnessed many of these

exhibits at their gardens at Inverewe, but you will also find a natural growth of lush vegetation and wild flowers at many points on your journey.

The beautiful Loch Maree

In the SW of Skye lies the hamlet of Elgol which has spectacular views over Loch Scavaig towards the Cuillin mountain range.

Opposite *The Isle of Skye lies off Scotland's NW coast and Portree is the island's capital.*

with the splendid heights of Slioch towering above it, leads south to the area of Torridon. From Gairloch to Kyle of Lochalsh is a land of incomparable mountains, lochs and seashore which come together with forests and moorland. The route is peppered with beautiful villages such as Plockton, Loch Carron, Applecross and Sheildaig, and

the high pass of Bealach nam Bo; a journey of 1 in 4 gradients and hairpin bends, while not being for the faint-hearted, provides staggering views across to the islands of Raasay and Skye.

From Kyle of Lochalsh the road leads south to Lochaber, past the picture-postcard Eilean Donan castle and through Kintail where the "Five Sisters" stand

proudly guarding the glen. The road leads high above the striking shores of Loch Garry, where the viewpoint gives a splendid vista across Invernessshire, and down to Invergarry.

To the south and west the land is remote and wild. The peninsulas of Knoydart, Moidart and Ardnamurchan (the most westerly point on the British mainland) represent some of the last wilderness areas left in Europe. Great, long sea lochs bite into the land from where enormous glaciers retreated at the end of the last ice age. Huge mountains tower from the shore and eagles circle overhead. Access into many of these remote glens is by foot, and therefore only for the fit and healthy visitor.

Scotland's west coast provides a staggering array of dramatic scenery where colours

Sheep farming is an important part of the Skye economy. Here sheep graze on the fertile grassy hillside near Quiraing (513m).

A view across Loch Eishort towards the mountains of Bla Bheinn (928m) and Garbh-bheinn (806m) from Ord, Isle of Skye.

change very quickly, and in the late summer spectacular sunsets disappear behind the islands of the Hebrides.

The Outer and Inner Hebrides bring romantic notions of peace and tranquility, and names such as Vatersay, Berneray and Rona fill these notions.

The Outer Hebrides; an archipelago of 70 or so miles, provides the first break in the Atlantic Ocean. The western seaboard, eternally pounded by huge rollers, is uncompromisingly beautiful. There are miles of broad, white, sandy beaches; the one on Barra is used as the runway for the plane service!

Apart from Harris, the Outer Hebrides are flat islands where crofting and fishing are still the mainstays of the economy.

The Inner Hebrides, sheltered as they are by their outer sisters, tend to be more fertile. They lie scattered down the coastline from Skye in the north to Islay in the south. Each island has its own charms; Skye with its historic links to Bonnie Prince Charlie and its magnificent Cuillin

The Pass of Glencoe in winter's grip. A solitary rowan tree holds on to the frozen rock to bloom again in Spring.

mountain range stretching across the southern shores: the magical "Small Isles" of Rhum, Eigg, Muck and Canna; fertile and wooded Mull whose main town, Tobermory, welcomes visitors in a colourful way; the green island of Jura, and neighbouring Islay where no less than seven distilleries each produces its own individual single malt whisky.

Fort William lies at the southernmost end of the Great Glen with Britain's highest mountain, Ben Nevis, towering paternally above the town. To the south is the famous "glen of weeping", Glencoe. It was here in 1692 that many of the clan MacDonald were murdered on a winter's night by their guests, the Campbells. Glencoe is a truly awe-inspiring place where you

Looking along Loch Eilside towards Ben Nevis, (1344m) the highest mountain in Britain.

Glenfinnan and Loch Shiel, the place where 1300 Highlanders raised the Stuart standard and joined Charles Edward Stuart to march south.

Opposite
A steam locomotive on the West Highland Line en route to Mallaig from Fort William.

climb through the gorge, with stark, rugged mountain peaks on either side, to reach the high open tracts of Rannoch Moor.

Continuing down the coast, the visitor enters Argyll and

A view from Oban looking over the Isle of Kerrera to the Isle of Mull beyond.

Opposite
15th century Kilchurn Castle by the shore of Loch Awe, Argyll.

follows the road down through the bustling town of Oban to the long, narrow peninsula of Kintyre. This beautiful countryside has the firth of Lorne to the west and the Clyde to the east. During the latter part of the last century and into the beginning of this one, many of the towns on Kintyre, the neighbouring island of Arran and towns on the mainland west

coast were favoured as holiday destinations by central belt inhabitants, thousands of whom would go "doon the watter" on great steam ships which plied the Clyde. Many of these towns still bear the distinctive architectural hallmarks of the Victorian era.

To the west, the Trossachs leads onto one of the main routes into Glasgow, and to the

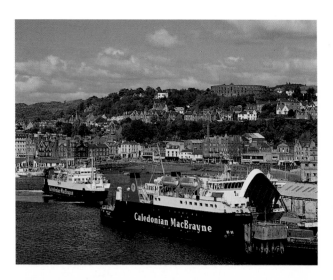

east to the town of Calendar and back to Stirling.

As Scotland's most populated city, Glasgow has a long established position as an important industrial centre, and was a major port with tobacco and textiles being the most important aspects of its economy in times past. Glasgow now has a growing reputation as a city of culture, providing homes for Scottish Opera, Scottish Ballet and the Scottish National Orchestra. In addition, its links with art through the architect and designer Charles Rennie MacKintosh, and the establishment of the famous Burrell Collection, means that Glasgow is a city not to be missed on any tour of Scotland.

The white sandy beaches of the Mull of Kintyre at Bellochantuy.

Summer on the Clyde estuary from Gourock looking towards Helensburgh and the distant hills around Loch Long and Loch Lomond.

Opposite
Oban Bay, Argyll and the CalMac passenger/car ferries to the isles.

Picturesque Tobermory on the Isle of Mull.

Highland cattle wade in the sea near Duart Castle, Isle of Mull.

A pastoral scene from the south of Loch Lomond looking towards Ben Lomond (974m).

Opposite

Scotland is also a country of fine shopping. The St Enochs Centre in the heart of Glasgow is an excellent example of modern town planning.

Evening falls over Old Kirkpatrick and the Erskine Bridge which carries traffic over the R Clyde.

The famous Turnberry Golf Course on the Ayrshire coast.

The last part of our journey through Scotland takes us south where the scenery is more rural and less dramatic. The coast road meanders to the town of Ayr; the leading holiday resort on the Firth of Clyde coast, famous for its premier Scottish racecourse, the reputation of nearby Troon golf course and its role as hub of Burns country - home of Scotland's most famous poet.

Sweetheart Abbey near Dumfries, founded in 1273.

The most southerly point on the Scottish mainland on the Mull of Galloway.

Opposite *The Ayrshire coast in the SW of Scotland near Dunure.*

At the southwest extreme of Scotland is the Mull of Galloway. Its splendid coastline offers sandy beaches alternating with stretches of rugged cliffs and occasional bays harbouring peaceful villages and ports. This area enjoys Scotland's mildest climate, bathing in the warmth of the Gulf Stream.

The most important town in the southwest is Dumfries. An attractive and bustling market town where farming is of major importance, it also provides a good base for exploring the many interesting historic sights and leisurely excursions such as Sweetheart Abbey, the last cistercian foundation in Scotland, or a trip round the Solway coast.

Scotland is a country of extremes; of high mountains and deep lochs, of bustling cities and peaceful villages, of great open expanses and intimate island life. Our wildlife is spectacular be it on the water, in the air or on land. We hope you have enjoyed this journey round Scotland, and that some of the photographs in this book will inspire you to visit more of our lovely country.

The heather clad slopes of Glen Trool in Dumfries and Galloway, where the memorial to Robert the Bruce, ancient King of Scots, can be visited.